Cadillac Men

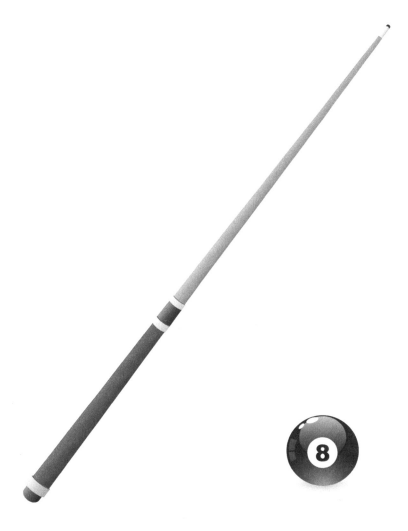

Other Books by Rebecca Schumejda

Falling Forward (sunnyoutside, 2009)
From Seed to Sin (Bottle of Smoke Press, 2011)
The Map of Our Garden (verve bath, 2009)
Dream Big, Work Harder (sunnyoutside, 2006)
The Tear Duct of the Storm (Green Bean Press, 2001)

Cadillac Men

Rebecca Schumejda

NYQ Books™

The New York Quarterly Foundation, Inc.
New York, New York

NYQ Books™ is an imprint of The New York Quarterly Foundation, Inc.

The New York Quarterly Foundation, Inc.
P. O. Box 2015
Old Chelsea Station
New York, NY 10113

www.nyqbooks.org

First Edition

Set in New Baskerville

Layout and Design by Raymond P. Hammond
Cover Illustrations by Hosho McCreesh | www.hoshomccreesh.com

Library of Congress Control Number: 2012948206

ISBN: 978-1-935520-68-9

Cadillac Men

Acknowledgments

A special thank you to Nathan Graziano and Lauren Restuccia for all of their assistance and support, also to my mother and husband for helping me find time to continue writing. A special thank you to Pauline Uchmanowicz, my mentor, for her ongoing support. Some of these pieces originally appeared in: *Calliope Nerve, Home Planet News, The Mas Tequila Review, New York Quarterly, Night Train, Outsider Writers, Rusty Truck, Trailer Park Quarterly, Thieves Jargon, Wilderness House Review, Words Dance, Zygote in my Coffee, 13 Miles from Cleveland.*

For Mark, My Cadillac Man
may the faint smell of gamble forever linger on our pillowcases

Contents

"The game of billiards has destroyed my naturally sweet disposition."

Mark Twain

Cadillac Men

Before 6 p.m., the pool hall's empty
besides the Chicago crew,
who still swear by
Cadillacs, Coltrane, and cheap cigars.

They're Vikings who look across the table,
their ocean, their starry night,
connecting balls like constellations,
mapping journeys while chalking up.

Every one of them has lost or found
his stroke between sunrise and sunset
in a pool room as dark and lonely
as the back pocket of a worn pair of denims.

At some point, they have all lost to the game:
a wife, a child, a home, friends,
self-respect, heirlooms, retirement, sanity.

They talk about the good ole days,
specific shots and calls made before I was born,
when so-and-so ran x number of balls
in a joint that no longer exists.

They're dinosaurs like the Cadillacs
they've been driving long before *The Hustler*
exploited the mechanics of the game.

They are Newton, Newman, and Neruda
blending physics, pool and poetry.
Their Cadillacs, as faithful as death,
are always right there waiting for them.

Crazy Eights, Kingston, NY

"It's better to buy a crappy piece of property in a good neighborhood than a mansion in a bad neighborhood. You can always rebuild a house, but you can't change a community."

my father's advice

Faith in Proverbs

Before the pool tables were assembled
or the sign hung from the building;
while I was still pregnant with our daughter
and visions of our future;
and you believed in the proverb:
If you build it they will come,
Cadillacs began orbiting the block
dragging their faith below them
like rusty mufflers scraping pavement.
Just like you and me, these men came to win.

The Table As a Classy Lady

On opening day, before the first pot of coffee's done brewing,
Shakes parks his baby blue Cadillac out front
then strolls in carrying a dusty pool case,
"Looks like I am out of retirement," he says.

He walks around the front table,
tips his Borsalino cap as if greeting a lady
then says, "Classy tables, really classy,
these are the kind of tables that drive men crazy."

Like Dust and Silence

Some men need no introduction,
they settle in like dust and silence
as if they were there before you
and will remain long after you're gone.

Wally The Whale walks into Crazy Eights
empty-handed, walks directly to the front table
and begins verbally scrutinizing each minute flaw.

After discussing his observations with Mark,
he turns around and walks out.

As I brush chalk from felt,
he grabs his case from his white Cadillac.

"This will work," he says when he comes back in,
"but we're gonna need a tight pocket table."

Social Darwinism

Two storefronts next to our pool hall, deemed unsafe by the city, still employ
drug dealers. Doors and windows, like rotten clams, are always open.

Expired work permits in filthy windows, like makeup on prostitutes,
give false hope.

Business owners, locked into leases, chug whiskey from coffee cups
and weigh options:
arson, suicide, bankruptcy, abandonment…

The guy at the clothing shop up the street resorted to selling bongs
and vaporizers, "for tobacco use only," to survive the recession
until his goods were commandeered.

The corner gas station's alcohol license is suspended again
for selling to underage kids.

This afternoon a lady walks into the pool hall alone and asks for money;
her baby needs formula.
When I say no, she says, "Fuck you then, bitch,"
slamming the door behind her.

"Baby, yeah right," Wally The Whale chuckles and shakes his head.

Some days more people come in to sell their stories than to buy table time.
Some days the landscape closes in on me like my father's superfluous advice.
Before the neighboring store closed down, the owners, all of their children,
and friends sat outside on plastic lawn chairs cursing, spitting,
and trying to sell used goods.
If they played electric guitars, it would be an *urban deliverance.*

When we opened the pool hall, I overheard the owner of the tattoo shop say,
"Oh God, there goes the neighborhood," as if we would be the city's downfall.

But today it doesn't matter because Wally's on the front pool table, and Lady Day's
singing "Speak Low" on the radio. I smile despite my father, who warned me:
It's all about location, location, location.

Table of Truth

Mikey Meatball's been kicked out
of every pool hall he's ever set foot in.
He's forged checks, harassed patrons,
hustled a small fortune, lost a small fortune.
Once he repeatedly rammed his car
into a guy's truck over a botched bet.

He's been locked up and drugged up.
He blames it all on Agent Orange.
In Vietnam he was an officer;
in Jersey he owned a billiard hall;
in Brooklyn, he owned an Italian delicatessen;
they called him "Papa Meatball."

In Texas, he played a man for his Cadillac
and won, but totaled it on his way back East.
On Haight-Ashbury,
he sold a hookah to a hippie for ten grand
claiming it was Jerry Garcia's.
In Connecticut, he siphoned gas
from some fish's car before
winning his wedding band on the table.

He's a regular in the police blotter,
most recently for whipping his dick out
at a bagel shop owner
for skimping him on cream cheese.
Once he convinced some kid
he shot like shit because
he was using a left-handed pool cue.
Last week, he told me he saw my husband
pick up a prostitute on Broadway,
just to see my jaw drop.
Instead, I responded,
"Well, at least he's getting some."

When Mikey looks into the table,
he sees his own version of reality:
fifteen object balls, six pockets,
and men who will believe anything
he says if there's money on the table.

Dizzy Gillespie's Cheeks

Aristotle comes in like air traveling from Dizzy Gillespie's cheeks
out through his trumpet. Quick to admit he's several months off Jenny,
estranged from the table and his children due to his most recent
incarceration, he's ready to bang some balls around a real table,
not one of those quarter bandits at the bar, all warped and worn.

He takes the back table and plays his version of straight pool.
While watching a basketball game, he coaches the players:
"Pass the goddamn ball, son. Puff, puff give, son," he yells.
"The hoop ain't no accessory, shoot, son, shoot!"

Outside the sun shines, people stop and look in the windows,
some come in to check the place out, they all say they'll be back.
Every now and then, Aristotle goes out for a cigarette,
he talks to everyone passing by. Each time he comes back in
he smiles and says, "Damn good day to be free, damn good."

Hours later, when Mark comes back with our daughter,
Aristotle's chops the *y* off my name as if it were a clumsy note,
"Hey Beck," he says, "she looks just like you."
He holds out a finger and my daughter wraps her hand around it.
"Damn," he laughs warm and rich like hot chocolate,
"she's got some grip, gonna be a hell of a pool player like her mommy."

Who Needs Television

Around noon,
the pool hall's empty
besides Wally,
who's practicing how
to miss shots.
I stare past his deception
out through the window.

Old Two-Shoes strolls past
pushing a mop and bucket.

A few seconds later,
the owner of the Chinese restaurant
down the street
runs after her screaming,
"What you doing?"

A minute later,
in slapstick tradition,
he walks by again,
pushing his mop and bucket.

Old Two-Shoes follows parroting,
"What you doing?"

A few minutes later,
a police car shadows
Old Two-Shoes,
who runs by cradling
a gold Buddha statue.

The owner of the Chinese restaurant
trails close behind
pointing at Old Two-Shoes
and yelling at the officer,
who refuses to get out of his car,
"What you doing?"

Rainy Day Abortion

A few blocks down from Crazy Eights,
in front of the women's health clinic,
a man holds a sign that reads:
"Pray to end abortion."
As if a dedicated employee,
he works the corner each day
from nine to five.
He stares down each woman
as if they are convicted murders,
even though many
are simply getting Pap smears.

Today, during a downpour,
I drive by to test
his commitment
only to find him
waiting out the storm
in the vestibule of the clinic
with his sign turned in
to his womb-less midsection
as if his beliefs
became a fetus he decided to abort.

Aristotle's Dream

With my daughter asleep in her stroller,
I play straight pool with Aristotle.
It's one o'clock on Monday.
A group of high school students
congregate around the quarter table.

"That ain't no table, son,"
Aristotle lectures one kid,
"now, this here's a table," he says,
running his slender, chocolate fingers
along the rail of the Brunswick
we're shooting on.

"You need to go back to school
and do some learning, damn.
Why ain't you there now anyway, son?"
The kids say it's Martin Luther King Day.
It's only September, but I keep quiet.

Aristotle chuckles, "I have a dream
that one day, even the city of Kingston,
a city sweltering with the heart of
oppression, will be transformed into
an oasis of freedom and justice."

The kids listen and watch us shoot,
then Aristotle shows one of them
how to better his bridge.
When the kids leave, Aristotle
looks right through me and snarls,
"Ain't nothing left of King's message
in Kings-ton."

Between the Sun and Me

for Mark

I stand outside the pool hall with you,
so I can steal drags from your cigarette
and discuss preparing the roses for winter,
even though stubborn leaves still cling to trees.
You tell me to stop rushing into the future,
then step in between me and the sun,
so I don't have to squint.
You wrap your hand around my forearm
and pull me toward you.

A man wearing a leather jacket
and shiny black shoes
startles us when he asks for cab fare.
He says his car broke down.
When you say no,
he asks if he can bum a smoke.
You open your pack, hand one over
and light it for him
just as Wally The Whale pulls up
and gets out of his Cadillac
holding his cue case.

"Hey Wally, what'cha got in there a gun?" the man asks.
Wally nods at you, winks at me
and ignores the man.

After a few seconds, the man backs away.
Wally mumbles about stupid junkies
as the man knocks on a door a few buildings down.
The door opens then slams shut on him.
He turns and walks down the street
in search of something or someone
who will stand in between him and the sun.

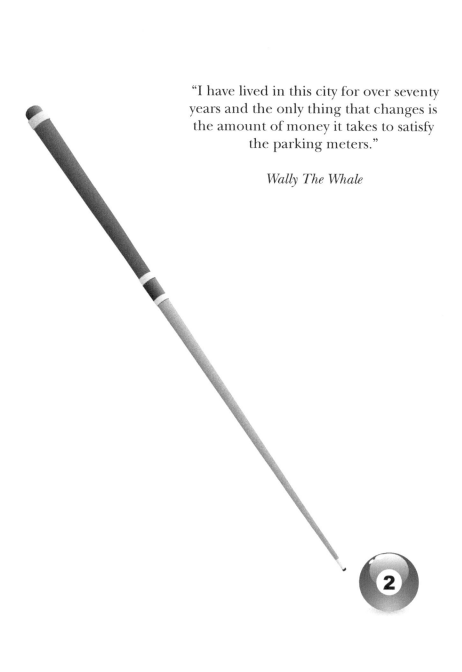

"I have lived in this city for over seventy years and the only thing that changes is the amount of money it takes to satisfy the parking meters."

Wally The Whale

After All, This Is a Bad Neighborhood

Spanish Fly's in the back,
banging around balls
as if they're fists
and the table's his punching bag.
His tight blue jeans are tucked into
his black cowboy boots;
his Hawaiian shirt
is respectfully tucked into his jeans.
Every now and then,
he licks his thumb and pinky,
smoothes out his mustache,
both fingers starting in the middle
then separating toward the ends.

He walks around the table
as if a horse is between his legs.
His nickname, self-proclaimed,
contradicts his outward appearance.
He's Japanese and stands five feet,
give or take a hair or two sticking
out from his mullet.

Spanish Fly loves classic rock.
Once, I saw him play a pool stick
as if it were a guitar
along with Jimi Hendrix's rendition of
the "Star-Spangled Banner,"
falling to his knees
as he struck the last chord.

Surprisingly, the men talk to him
about their ailing love lives
and listen to his advice.
He tells Shakes:
that he needs to stop looking for a mother
and to read the Kama Sutra.

He tells Aristotle:
to get rid of his incarcerated woman
and to use more cologne.
He tells Mikey:
that beating his wives directly correlates
with his high divorce rate.

Without prompting,
he tells my husband,
in reference to me:
watch that one, she's trouble.
When my husband's not around,
he tells me *watch that one, he's trouble,*
then winks on his way out.

I watch as he prepares to ride off.
He puts on his helmet
before jumping onto his twelve-speed bicycle.

Jenny

Whenever Aristotle comes in, he takes the back table,
turns on a basketball game, asks: "What's new, Beck?"
Some days he plays quietly, says he's
soul searching; other days he gives sermons.

Today he talks about how his woman is coming home.
She's been gone a long time, but she writes beautiful letters
from her cell, real poetry, the kind that makes bars melt.

I agree to play straight with him to 100 and he lets me break.
"Her name's Jenny, right?" I ask and he laughs and laughs.
"No Beck, but Jenny is the only woman that will never leave me."
"Where is she now?" I ask and he laughs so hard
I think he's going to fall right out of his skin.

He leans on the table and catches his breath before saying,
"She's probably being sold down the street right now, Beck."
He turns back to the table, shakes his head and runs me out.

Bobby Balls-In-Hand

I.

By six, Bobby Balls-In-Hand is down grocery money.

By seven, a month without gas and cigarettes.

He chalks his stick between each shot,
uses a plethora of tissues to wipe
sweat and chalk dust from his hands.

By ten, he's down rent.

By eleven, he's writing an IOU.

II.

The men say he got his moniker
because he can't keep Whitey on the table,
but during a lull between songs,
he kneels in front of the ball return
to pick up an abandoned nickel.
As if in confession, he speaks hesitantly:

Once I was married to a beautiful woman.
We had a beautiful little girl.

But you know I can't resist a money game
even if I know I'll lose.

When she couldn't wait up anymore, she left,
no note,
no forwarding address,
no further contact.

So, that's how I really got my name,
my wife left me
with my fucking balls in my hand.

Something Better

All day I search for words;
I want to write a beautiful poem.

The Butcher, alone at the front table,
slices all the balls in without blinking.

Because I understand this,
I want to sculpt him into syllables.

I study his form,
the contours of his experiences,
painfully elegant.

As he draws back the seven ball,
I consider him cast in bronze,
balancing the bulkiness of his decisions.

Pensive like a ballerina
grappling with gravity, a Degas.

Once he sacrificed his marriage
for one dance with a lovely lady.

He told me that those are risks you take
when you believe there's something better.

Rosary Beads and Pool Balls

When the army
couldn't salvage
Shake's soul,
his mother's fingers
kept track of Hail Marys
and Our Fathers
recited over decades
for her wayward son.

But no wooden beads
could save him
from the old ivories,
so she stayed awake
waiting for him,
sometimes for days.
When he came in,
she'd fix him a meal,
ask him when
he was going to find
a good woman
and settle down.

He'd kiss her forehead
and tell her he could
never find a woman
as good as her.
This made everything alright,
until she was waiting again.

After she passed,
Shakes started going
to church religiously.
He hung her rosary beads
from the rearview mirror
of his Cadillac.
Whenever the beads tap
against the windshield,
it sounds like pool balls
in the distance
calling him home.

Fall and Men

Since he didn't have a moniker,
but deserved one,
Mark and I took to calling him Ebenezer Scrooge
when he couldn't hear us,
then Ebenezer,
and finally just Eby.

He doesn't like foreigners, kids, black people,
women, people who talk too loud,
rich people, poor people, happy people, sad people,
people who talk when he's concentrating
and this fucking recession.

Today he is particularly perturbed by Spanish Fly,
who took the table next to him
and is singing "Welcome to the Jungle,"
above the Dave Brubeck CD that's playing.

Whenever Spanish Fly needs to take a shot
from the area between their tables,
Eby gets in his way.
Spanish Fly doesn't seem to mind,
he just steps aside, sings and watches,
which of course pisses Eby off more.

I walk outside to take a call,
so they won't hear me pleading with bill collectors,
and notice all the leaves have fallen from the trees.
Through the windows,
I watch the two men, Eby and Spanish Fly,
practicing on separate tables.

So much has gone by unnoticed lately:
like words I didn't take the time to write down
or say; like days that turned into months
without laughter; like the distance growing
between you and I; so quick men wake up

fallen
angry
and alone.

The Regulars at Crazy Eights

There are men who bet
their paychecks on the flip
of a single card;
mortgage their homes
for a roll of the bones;
chance their car keys
on the nine in the side pocket.

Many of these men go
to church on Sundays and pray
for a big win next time,
for their wives to return,
or for their children to be luckier.

Penniless, these men
throw stones in collection plates.
They come to the pool hall
in lieu of confession
and look to my husband
for absolution.

These men troll the tables
with baited smiles.
Their eyes open like hymnals—
so wide, like the holes
in their stories,
that you can fall
through them
and never hit the ground.

Names, Faces and Tunnels

Terry charges in and up to the counter.
I introduce myself as Becky.
The first half-dozen times
when he calls me Rachel
I correct him, after that I let it slide.
Names and faces escape me too.

He tells me his wife's name is Rachel too
and I am as beautiful as she is.

Outside storm clouds move as quickly as Terry,
they make it feel like we're entering and exiting
the Lincoln Tunnel over and over again.

He asks if we have an 8-ball team,
and I say, "Yeah, we have a few spots open,
but you'll have to come back when my husband, Mark,
is around. He'll be in later tonight."

The wind that blows our store's sign
makes me nervous, the way faces and tunnels do.

Without invitation,
Terry picks up the newspaper
fanned out on the counter,
he flips to the classifieds and says,
"Damn, every week there are less jobs."

When he turns around to leave,
we are back inside the tunnel.
Rain pours from the sky
like molasses, like debt, like regret.
"Fuck," he says,
"I left my wife's car window open.
Nice meeting you Rachel.
Tell your husband I'll be back later."

The Stubborn Umbrella

When Terry comes back,
he brings his wife, Rachel,
who wears a floral muumuu,
carries a pool case in one hand,
and holds an umbrella in the other.
While she struggles to close her umbrella,
I wonder why her hair's soaking wet.

I point them out to Mark.
Terry extends his hand
then pulls back awkwardly
trying to conceal a bandage on his arm.

"I know this doesn't look good,
but I can still shoot; I was a six in league
before the accident. Wanna play?" he asks.

Rachel gives up on the umbrella,
leaves it open in the front corner of the store
and wobbles in farther.
When she sees the stroller,
she walks toward my daughter.

She peeks in to see my daughter squirming
and smiles until she notices
my eyes accidentally tripping over
the rotten tree stumps
rooted in her muddy mouth.
She closes her trembling lips.
"Do you have kids?," I ask.
She nods yes, fighting a smile.

Mark places a set of balls on the front table
and while Terry racks,
he pushes a button on Rachel's umbrella
and it collapses with ease
like a house of cards blown over by a breeze.

Rachel looks up in the air,
so I can't see her teeth
and says "Thanks, you're lucky."
Not sure if she is talking to me or Mark,
I say thank you.

We Were All This Small

Rachel never did call me by my name
or smile in front of me again,
but Terry continued to call me Rachel,
even after Mark corrected him multiple times.

Within a few weeks,
we found out more than we wanted,
but less than we needed to know
about Terry and Rachel.

Sadness bunched up around Terry
like the flab around Rachel's waist
and flopped around
where everyone could see it.

I learned it wasn't rainwater
that drenched Rachel's hair that day;
it was a permanent oily residue
that made it appear
as if she always
just walked in from the rain.

No matter how sunny it was out,
Terry couldn't see past his misery,
an angry cloud that followed him
around like his own shadow.

Whenever Rachel was in the pool hall,
she gravitated to my daughter
and the candy bars in the vending machine.
Once, while she cradled my daughter,
with her mouth full of chocolate,
she mumbled: *It's hard to believe*
we were all this small and pure.

Balloons

While Rachel chain-chews Baby Ruth bars,
she tells me she hates balloons.

I ask her to keep an eye on my daughter, so I can spook the kid
who steals beef jerky sticks then eats them in our bathroom.
I take the container of beef jerky and put it under the counter.

"Balloons?" I ask when I come back over,
a thin string of chocolate drips from the corner of her mouth.

She stares down the pink balloon
tied to the handle of my daughter's stroller
that the lady next store gave us.

"They're dangerous," she murmurs.
"You mean if you choke on them?" I ask.

"I need a drink," she says staring at the balloon.
I go back over to the counter, pour a few shots of whiskey
into two coffee cups, come back, hand her one and sip the other.

"So balloons," she speaks slowly, drinks quickly,
uses her fingers to dislodge caramel from the sides of her mouth,
waits; I grab her cup and mine, fill them both to the brim with more whiskey.

When I get back, she is staring at my daughter.
I hand her the cup and she says,
"My daughter was only a few months older than yours.
I brought her with me to the store to buy balloons for her birthday party.
There were about twenty balloons, all the colors of the rainbow.
I put them in the passenger seat of my car and thought it would be fine.
I could sorta see out the window and I was just going down the road.
I was talking to her, telling her how much fun we were gonna have,
about the cake I made, the streamers I would hang
and about how I couldn't believe she was already a year old.
Then there was this noise, this screeching, snapping, and cracking.
All I remember was coming in and out and the balloons

were right there in my face. There was yelling about getting us out.
There was a machine cutting, grinding and squealing,
but none of those balloons popped:
a few of them wiggled to freedom and flew up into the sky;
I suspect in the same way my daughter's spirit did."

"I am sorry," I say. She says it was a long time ago,
she never did tell anyone else from around here except Terry.

"I am so sorry," I say as I get up to get us more whiskey
and a pair of scissors. I return, hand Rachel her drink,
then cut the string of the balloon and walk outside to let it go.

A mix of rain and snow pelt the balloon,
slowing it down, as it rises over the city.

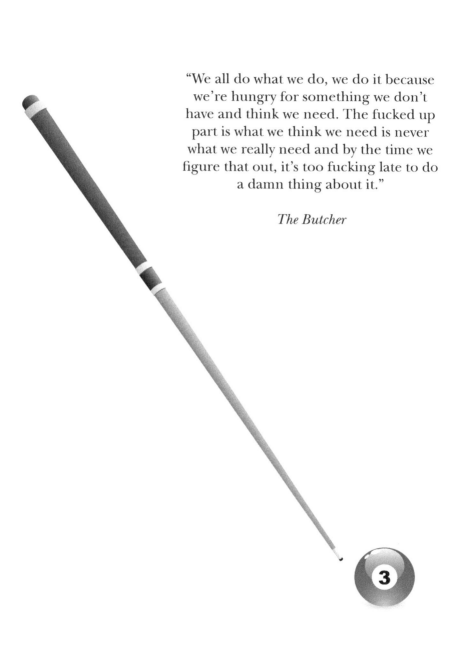

"We all do what we do, we do it because we're hungry for something we don't have and think we need. The fucked up part is what we think we need is never what we really need and by the time we figure that out, it's too fucking late to do a damn thing about it."

The Butcher

Optical Illusions

Through the pool hall windows,
I watch slush collect
at the street's midline and hips.
The snow can't hold its shape
like a defeated woman.

Outside, struggling business owners
salt sidewalks with fistfuls
of broken dreams,
so the ghosts, prostitutes, and
drug dealers don't slip.

This side of town wears down
people's words;
passersby only grunt
if their eyes meet.

Inside, The Butcher plays down
his game, hoping the new guy
will challenge him.

With a straight face,
he asks me a basic 9-ball rule.
Knowing pool etiquette,
I answer without looking up
from the book I pretend to read.

A snow plough redistributes slush.
It's only 7:30, snowflakes falling
under streetlights are lonely women
disappearing quietly
like all the legitimate businesses
on this street.

Old Two-Shoes stares
into the front windows
as if they are carnival mirrors;
she gasps at her own reflection.

49

When the new guy drops
a crisp one hundred dollar bill
on the table, The Butcher says,
"Well…ah…I don't know
how 'bout twenty and table time?"
The new guy racks.

By ten, The Butcher's down two hundred
and begging, "Oh come on man,
one more, my wife's gonna kick me out
if I can't make rent. Double or nothing?"
The Butcher racks.

By midnight the slush turns to ice.
Cars that usually accelerate
through this part of town,
are forced to slow down.

The Butcher turns the tables;
he is up two hundred
and acting like a school girl
discovering the power of her tits.

Later, when The Butcher
pulls into his driveway,
he swears he sees his wife
waiting at the window,
but it's just snowflakes
stuck to his eyelashes,
icy and thick like his lies.

The Corner Chop Shop

Before chain supermarkets,
women went to *The Corner Chop Shop*
to select cuts of meat.
With their children in tow,
they flirted
for the juiciest cut
and smiled as if they were special
when The Butcher handed over
thin-sliced ham
to keep their children quiet.

Pickled pigs feet, eggs,
and homemade beef jerky
in large glass jars
were simple pleasures.

Wally The Whale
used the walk-in as his office.
He conducted business
in between racks of
hanging carcasses.
He wrapped cash
in butcher paper
and lucky men walked out
with their winnings
under both arms.

Men sat around tables
draped with red-and-white-checkered cloths.
They'd sip espresso and talk about
last night's game or fight.
Back then, everyone knew each other.
Back then, there were three pool halls
in this town and
The Butcher was a lucky man.

Now there are five supermarkets
and one dying pool hall in this town.
The Butcher shoots pool all afternoon
then heads off to the bars to forget:
his forced retirement, alimony,
and deteriorating heart.

One time, while playing 9-ball
with my husband, The Butcher confessed
that sometimes he walks down meat aisles
just to poke holes in the plastic wrap
that imprisons precut beef.
This is all the energy he has left for revenge.

Flat Rocks

It's the first Saturday night
after the winter electric bills arrived,
the pool hall's as empty
as our bank accounts and the city streets.

We stand outside,
so Mark can smoke cigarettes
and skip thoughts
like flat rocks into the air.

He drapes his jacket
over my shivering shoulders
then reminds me that it's too late
to winterize the roses,
but he says we can try anyway,
we don't have much to lose.

When I turn around,
the store windows
look like a body of water
reflecting our drowning bodies,
all the empty tables
mock us like lifeboats
just out of our reach.

Sober on a Snowy Day

Outside, cars tiptoe
through snow.
Aristotle's on table four
and his soapbox again,
talking about how he
sees things, you know.
He says that prison
does that to a person,
makes them sober
on a snowy day.

He stirs air,
thick like old coffee,
with the tip of his cue
and launches off
into a dramatic monologue
about social injustices.

The men playing
on the next table
listen with their eyes.
Outside a truck
throws salt onto icy streets
and men wrapped up
in financial depression
walk past on their way
to the closest bar.

On the radio, Thelonious Monk
attacks piano keys, backs off,
then returns; his silences
are silly little tricks
that make Aristotle nervous.

Even though he's on step four,
Aristotle sneaks out to his car
to shotgun a beer

and smoke a cigarette.
Back inside,
he uses the shadow
of his stick to line up shots.
When he misses,
he leans into the table
and whispers inaudibly
to his ghost opponent.

Once he likened his life
to a snow globe that
some stupid motherfucker
keeps picking up and shaking.
I like that metaphor, I really do
like that metaphor.

Gettysburg Address

Aristotle's on the back table,
holding his stick up in the air, between shots,
as if it were a javelin.
Infuriated, he rambles about social injustices
then flips his cue stick upside down
and uses the butt as a microphone:
"Fourscore and seven beers ago,
our forefathers brought forth
on this continent, a nation contradicted
by liberty, and dedicated to the prostitution
of all men disillusioned about being created equal."

Unfazed, Wally The Whale continues his run.
Mikey Meatballs and Bobby Balls-In-Hand
look over at him, then at me, then back at him.
A teenager at the quarter table
asks his friend why Aristotle's words
sound so familiar.
Shakes, who just walked in,
looks at Mikey and says,
"Maybe I got somewhere else to be today."
Mikey smirks then says,
"This is why Lincoln got shot."

After a few minutes,
Aristotle stops, twists his face
and body, looks around as if
he doesn't know where he is
then stumbles into the bathroom.
Everyone, besides Wally and me,
speculate then fall silent.
When Aristotle emerges,
about an hour later,
calm and collected, he yells to me,
"Hey, Beck, you got a motherfucking plunger?"

Frozen

Bobby Balls-In-Hand marches in, takes out his stick, twists it together tightly.
Before he takes off his red scarf or says hello, he chalks up.
"You better throw some salt down on the sidewalk before someone falls
and busts their ass," he says as he grabs a set of balls.

Bobby shoots straight pool on the front table, as I rock
my infant daughter; Billie Holiday tells us *What a little moonlight can do...*
When I catch Bobby playing peek-a-boo with my daughter, he blushes through
his confession: "I believe my own daughter's 'bout eighteen by now."

Shakes pulls up in his Cadillac. Within five minutes, the bet's made
and Bobby's breaking. Holding my sleeping daughter in one arm,
I go outside to toss salt over ice. I watch the owner of the Chinese restaurant
stumble over a bank of snow. People walk by without looking at him.

Before they're even warmed up, Bobby and Shakes argue over whether
the three ball's frozen against the rail. They call me over and I say it's not.
Annoyed with my call, Shakes throws twenty on the table, promising he'll
never play Bobby again, then he walks out, his last words to Bobby
a round of stuttered curses frozen in the air.

Knowledge

On the other end of the line,
a young girl asks:
Does Bobby Miller play pool there?
When I counter: *Who's this?*
a few silent seconds pass
before she hangs up.

I go back to playing
9-ball with Diego,
who snaps his castanet fingers
and says "Nice shot, nice shot,"
no matter how easy the setup.

Then it registers:
that could have been
Bobby's daughter,
who he hasn't seen in
over seventeen years.
I wonder if my question
answered hers or if she
really doesn't want to know.

Later in the afternoon
when Bobby Balls-In-Hand comes in,
I don't look up when he grabs
the balls from the counter.
The entire time he plays Diego,
I weigh why I should tell him
against why I shouldn't.

After his inevitable loss,
he asks me to change a hundred.
I look over his shoulder
at the 9x4½ reason why
he doesn't know his own daughter
as I hand back four twenties,
a ten and two fives.

Several minutes after he leaves,
the sky turns gray and sleet moves in
to fill that empty silence
that doesn't owe anything to anyone.

The Art of Dumping

The storm dumped a foot of snow
on top of the city, effortlessly.
In a yard across from the pool hall,
three boys manipulate snow
into a hulking polar bear;
they place a pair of black sunglasses
over its eyes and a Coca-Cola can
into its right paw. Passersby stop
in admiration, some come back
with cameras to pose beside the bear.

Misfortune dumps Mikey Meatballs
on our doorstep, chuckling;
he walks around the pool hall
in search of the perfect house cue.
He places potential sticks on tables
and rolls them back and forth.
As a dumping aficionado,
he lives the rule: never let anyone
see you play your true speed,
especially your wives.

Snowplows, backers, and
divorce lawyers clean up sloppy messes.
There is an art to dumping
that takes into account temperature,
touch, and timing. Some men get rich
on other men's losses.

When Dee arrives, snow turns to rain;
the stake is placed behind the register.
As the temperature rises,
I watch the sunglasses slip
from the bear's snout,
the Coca-Cola can drop from its paw
and Mikey Meatballs eat Dee's lunch.

Ten Winters and Counting

for Mark

You wore faded jeans,
ripped at the knees,
and that fluorescent-blue ski jacket
I threw away
    "accidentally"
        as soon as we moved in together.

You walked slowly around the pool table.
Your chiseled face, Picasso Cubist,
    under the swaying light
        accentuated your lazy eye.

After I slid quarters in,
    you racked the balls;
it didn't matter that it was your table.

Later when you
    "accidentally"
scratched on the eight,
    you extended your hand,
so cold, I shivered.

Tonight, winter approaching
    you remind me
        about that jacket,
    thrown away years ago.

I loved that jacket,
    it was the warmest jacket
        that I ever owned
you've told me
    every winter since,

ten years and counting.

Valentine's Day

Cable network runs
The Godfather movies
back-to-back on Valentine's Day
for men like Mikey Meatballs
and Bobby Balls-In-Hand.

They watch between shots
and quote lines in unison:
"You sonofabitch, do you know
who I am? I'm Moe Greene!
I made my bones when you
were going out with cheerleaders."

Last night, Mark informed me
that Valentine's Day
is a synthetic holiday,
placed between Christmas and Easter
to boost the economy.

Trying to be original,
I lean against the counter,
and press my pen down on
a ninety-nine cent card.

In response to Mark's aversion
to the establishment's scams,
I search for words, rich in romance,
to change his convictions,

just as Mikey Meatballs belches,
startling my fingers
into a misguided line
that I salvage into an arrow
piercing a lopsided heart.

"You don't know shit about playing pool until you figure out where the hell the game and the players are taking you."

Wally The Whale

Where the Game Takes You

It's Tuesday
        snow falls
                like deceit.
                Snowplows passing
        echo balls rolling down rails.

Shakes strolls in wearing plastic grocery bags over his shoes.
He takes down his umbrella, unzips his coat,
before removing the bags that he hangs over a chair
        to drip dry.

"Hi ya, how's the action?"
        I look up from the sad table, smiling. "Quiet."

He knows and I know, he's looking for Mikey Meatballs.
        I pick up the phone and ring Mikey
                then put on a fresh pot of coffee
                because somehow I've been demoted to secretary.

While he waits, we play a game of straight to fifty; he spots me half.
                Wally The Whale shows up, goes behind the counter
                        to grab his stick and a set of Centennials.
                "Hey Wally, how's things?" Shakes asks.

Wally nods, chalks up, leans into a break. He chips one in at a time
        like Michelangelo. His body language quotes the celebrated artist:
                "If people knew how hard I worked to get my mastery,
                        it wouldn't seem so wonderful at all."
                This is where the game took him.

After running four, Wally smiles. "It's your bridge," he coaches,
        repositioning my self-doubting fingers. "See."
                I run three more then scratch.

Mikey's mouth moseys in before he does;
        the duck, duck, goose game's up;
                the stake's set;

65

Mikey's mouth runs unpunctuated right through Shake's patience.

Eventually, Mikey and the snow let up, just enough and Shakes
    absconds without
goodbyes, leaving two plastic bags hanging, like deflated
    breasts, over the empty chair.

On With This Sad Day

When Unlucky Louie walks into the pool hall,
he always greets me with,
"Hey honey, I'm home."
If he's got work on the horizon,
he's relatively happy and if not
he usually talks about moving out of town.
Most of the time, he's mentally packing.

Today, Unlucky Louie's pool stick betrays him,
the way my body has done to me lately.
After cursing the balls for ten minutes,
he packs up, but pays for the full hour,
bringing me up to date on his world.

His neighbors kept him up all night
and their cats sprayed his welcome mat.
His landlord won't fix the leaky roof,
so he lets the rainwater collect
in empty paint cans
that stain circles onto his carpet.

His boys play video games day and night,
eat all his food and drink his whiskey;
they don't work and won't shovel the walkway;
and he's tired, so tired of this damn town.

And he can't shoot for shit and he's gonna retire,
and the women at the bars aren't the same anymore;
no one wants to have good clean fun;
no one wants to go out dancing;
no one wants to listen to anyone anymore.
So he stays home to watch the boob tube.

When he's done with his tirade,
he leans into the counter and asks,
"How are you doll? And the little one?"
He's the only one who asks sincerely.
For this, I want to tell him the truth

about how my body has turned against me
since the birth of my daughter and how I love
her so much, but at the same time long
for my old-self, before the tearing and scarring
of motherhood and the surgeries that have
only made it worse, but no man wants to hear
about these kinds of grievances;
these bodily sacrifices women make;

and men don't want to share their honest heartaches;
the loneliness that settles down next to them in bed
where their wives are or were
because then we would all know
each other intimately and we wouldn't be able to
escape into our own private, sad days.

Wheeling and Dealing

After losing a dozen or so games of 9-ball to Mikey, Spanish Fly's penniless.

"All I got left, Mikey, is my bike and my cowboy boots."

Mikey hesitates. "I'll play you for the boots," he grins.

The snow falling stalls his decision.

"Well, I am wearing wool socks. I want twenty balls in straight. If I win, I get that beater car of yours," Spanish Fly points to the Mistubishi Mikey just picked up at an auction.

"How about fifteen? I'll probably get more mileage out of your boots than that Japanese piece of shit anyhow," Mikey snickers.

"I'd bet you your wife, but she's more beat up than your car," Spanish Fly says as he racks.

By the end of the hour, Mikey's trying to squeeze his bulbous feet into Spanish Fly's cowboy boots. Chuckling, he says, "Don't you wish we were bowling?"

Spanish Fly pushes out into the snow, but within seconds runs back in screaming: "Some dumb, motha fuckin' crackhead stole my goddamn bicycle tires."

Wool Socks

I.

After someone stole Spanish Fly's wheels,
we let him bring his bicycle inside.
He came in a little less for awhile,
once inside he always took off
his new sneakers, and played in his wool socks.

On a day when melting snow
mingled with street filth
creating a mixture resembling gravy,
Mikey took to calling him Wheels,
and the new moniker stuck around
like all the trash-talk does in this broken city.

Wheels's gait and advice on love wavered;
his stroke possessed less life
like Mikey clogged the arteries
of his stick and slowed down his play.

II.

But pool players have their seasons too,
and today Wheels struts in, takes off
his new cowboy boots, exposing a raggedy hole
in one of his old wool socks
that his big toe peeks out through.

I finally understand his old moniker,
how a woman could stick to him
like fly tape as he leans his ride
against the pinball machine and
removes his stick from its case
as if it were a samurai sword.
Before Wheels breaks, Mikey pulls up
in his Caddy as if by telepathy.
He strides in like Minnesota Fats, not

70

Gleason's character in *The Hustler,*
but Rudolf Walter Wanderone, Jr.,
the man who built his fame
from Tevis's character.
With striking resemblance,
Mikey's mouth moves at the speed of light.

"I got my army with me, Wheels,
wanna play? Even when you lose,
I'll buy ya a new pair of socks."

Wheels smiles, "Sure thing, a little nine?"

The wager is whispered.
Mikey snorts at the proposal,
shakes on it, smiling at his invisible audience,
making pot shots at his pigeon
until he is far behind.

Wheels doesn't say a word,
just dances around the table
in his frayed wool socks.

After making the winning ball,
Wheels turns to me and asks,
"Do you have a carjack and lug wrench?"

Outside one at a time,
Spanish Fly removes the wheels
from Mikey's Cadillac then rolls each tire
down the street to the place where
he lays his head down to rest each night.

Because a Smart Man Can Dignify a Lousy Moniker

After losing his tires, Mikey Meatballs never called Spanish Fly Wheels again,
but everyone else did with smirks on their faces.

Mikey's Caddy sat on its knees, like a defeated man,
for a week before he finally came back for it.

Mikey said he took his ex-wife, Patty, to the Bahamas for a long weekend,
but I saw her at the grocery store during their trip.

Wheels instantly gained honorary Cadillac Man status.

Wally The Whale gave him a Cadillac emblem, which
Wheels proudly mounted on the handlebars of his twelve-speed.

A smart man can make a lousy moniker dignified;
he can make the felt on the table his armor, the cue stick his sword.

Evening the Score

Wheels comes in a few days later,
he hands me a Polaroid snapshot
of four tires stacked beside a couch.

On top of the tires is a piece of plywood.
Void of expression, he asks:
"Do you like my new coffee table?"

On His Handlebars

I.

Not long after Spanish Fly
became Wheels
and Mikey Meatballs hit Patty
in the face with a nine ball,
Wheels started kicking around
with Rita, who worked
at the beauty parlor
a few blocks down.

From time to time,
he'd bring her in to play,
but mostly she just watched TV,
and pulled bubblegum
from her mouth
and twisted it
around and around
her long, curly, neon,
acrylic fingernails.

II.

So tonight, when Rita's
in the restroom
and Wheels and The Butcher
are playing 9-ball,
I overhear Wheels say
he's playing for a ring.
It doesn't take long
before Wheels is up
and The Butcher
tries to convince him
to double it for the diamond,
which of course
goes over Rita's teased bangs.

III.

So Wheels agrees
and wins again and again.
A few hours after close,
The Butcher pays up
and tips me
for waiting around.

Wheels, two Gs richer,
grabs his lady, his stick
and his ride,
walks out into
the windy streets.
He holds the bike
while Rita steadies
herself on top
of his handlebars.
With the Cadillac emblem
suggestively pressed
against her crotch,
they ride off triumphantly.

When the Hustler Gets Hustled

I.

Since word and lightning
travel in front of
hustlers and thunder,
The Butcher knows
all about Mikey Meatballs.

So when Mikey's around
he chops sloppily at the balls
as if they're beef scraps
instead of prime rib
then brags about how
his stroke is coming back.

Alone on Tuesday mornings,
The Butcher thinly slices
each shot, scarcely missing a cut.
Sometimes he gives away
little pieces of himself;
because his daughter's my age,
he slips and calls me Mary.

His Cadillac was taken away
by the repo man a few years back,
right after he was forced
to close up shop.

Recently, The Butcher sold
his Brunswick because
it couldn't fit into
the tiny apartment he was
forced into after divorce.

The man who stole his wife
called about the classified ad
and tried to talk him down
on the price of the table.

II.

So today when
Mikey Meatballs strolls in,
it's not hard for The Butcher
to look vulnerable,
limping about in his misery.
And Mikey's been waiting for this
because he knows The Butcher's
a Cadillac Man
who drives a Dodge Neon
and he thinks
he's down on his luck
and shooting like shit.

"You wanna play straight for a hundred?" Mikey asks.
The Butcher hesitates.
"What will you give me?" He finally counters.
"Ten balls in a race to 100," Mikey offers.

The Butcher nods and Mikey racks.
It isn't until the end
that The Butcher comes alive,
still losing by twenty balls.
He sighs and pays up.

III.

"Hey, Mary can you put on a fresh pot of coffee?" he asks me.

IV.

Before the coffee's brewed,
the new bet's quadrupled.
After his first thirty-ball run,

The Butcher's smiling past
Mikey's sexist jokes
and ridiculous stories
at the man he was
when this town was his,
when his Cadillac waited outside
obediently like his wife,
who always had dinner and
an icy mug of beer on the table
by seven sharp.

When Mikey's down fifty balls,
The Butcher sips his cheap coffee
as if it were espresso.
The table is his again
and the balls are lucky numbers
called by the pocket one after the other.

When The Butcher leaves,
he hands me a hundred
and says: "Hey Mary, keep the change for a rainy day."

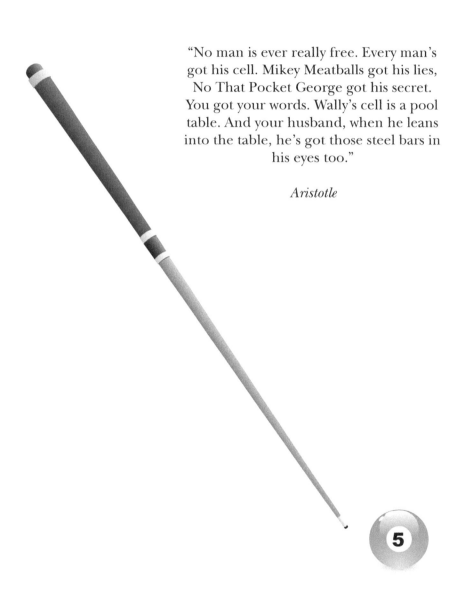

"No man is ever really free. Every man's got his cell. Mikey Meatballs got his lies, No That Pocket George got his secret. You got your words. Wally's cell is a pool table. And your husband, when he leans into the table, he's got those steel bars in his eyes too."

Aristotle

Atomic Bombs

"Nothing in life is to be feared, it is only to be understood."
—*Marie Curie*

As I brush chalk from felt,
the men at the front table
compare and contrast wars:
World War II, Vietnam and Iraq.
I overhear atomic bombs,
and think of Marie Curie,
who won not just one
but two Nobel Prizes.

In the foggy haze
of blue chalk dust,
I wonder what contributions
any of us in this pool hall
will make in our lifetimes?
Wasting our days with pool
and poetry will surely not
end any war or improve
the quality of lives.

Oh Marie, if you were here
shooting at high balls,
what would you think
when Mikey Meatballs screams:
"I killed a Goddamn gook
just to watch him bleed?"
Would you cringe at my poems
filled with self-pity?

As a child, a scuttle of coal
was your hope diamond.
As a college student,
you survived on bread,
tea and an occasional egg.

At the Sorbonne in Paris,
you were one of two women
amongst more than
a thousand men.
Did they snicker
when you slipped into
your lab coat?

Oh Marie, if you were here now
eyeing the eight, getting ready
to make a bank shot,
what would you say when
Mikey brags about holding a gun
to his ex-wife's head
because the bitch asked him
to bring out the garbage again
or when Shakes says
that the only thing women
are good for is procreation?

Widowed, you raised two children
alone, fixed their meals,
combed knots from their matted hair,
and tucked them in
before returning to your work.
When Eve wore too much makeup
and Irene married a man
you disapproved of—
you worried.

How I admire your selflessness—
the tragedy of your death:
overexposure to the same element
you isolated;
the same element
that destroys cancer
killed you and one of your daughters.

But still your findings
have survived you.

Oh Marie, if you were here
holding a cue stick in your hands
observing our contributions to mankind,
what would you say now
as Mikey Meatballs waves
his arms feverishly behind him
and announces that he just dropped
another atomic bomb?

Chalk Dust

No That Pocket George
is in the backroom,
snorting cocaine
straight from the rail
in between shots.

No one tells him
about the blue chalk
on the bridge
of his nose;
instead they let him win,
so he cuts generous lines.

When it's all gone,
they'll stop laughing
at his stories
and they'll start
shooting.

The Pool Table, a Shallow Pond

One night, after hours at the bar
down the road, No That Pocket George
stumbles in to tell me about how
his brother drowned in a shallow pond
when they were playing hide and seek.

His mother never forgave him, so now
      he hits the balls harder than he should
            and thinks of his mother's apron,
                  the one she always wore
                      even on the day her son
              was buried behind the old barn;

the apron she wore when she waded
      into the shallow pond
            and fished out her youngest son,
                who was face down in the murky water;
the apron she wore
      when she screamed
            I hate you
      into a callous sky because George was hiding
              under the porch.

He whacks the cue ball, a white apron,
as hard as he can because
sometimes after he plays too long,
the cloth on the table is algae
masking a shallow pond.
And sometimes after he drinks too much
beer foam looks like that film
sitting on a shallow pond.
And when there's a full apron in the night sky,
he is that little boy hiding under the porch.

The Table Swallows Wally The Whale

The table swallows Wally like poetry does to me,
    takes us away from the day's drudgery:
        paying the bills, worrying about what will break next,
    and where we'll get the money to fix it.

Fifteen object balls
    spread out   across the felt;
        twenty-six letters
           in the alphabet;
we both dream
    of possibilities,   combinations,   perfect breaks.

He spends afternoons
    practicing how to miss a shot;
        while I pick apart words   to resurrect.
We both have our own language:
    underappreciated
        and misunderstood.

We both struggle with rules.
    I hold my pen with the same intensity
        he does his cue.
           Felt and paper
              obstacles
                we navigate.

It's when writing swallows me that I understand
    his Captain Ahab-ish obsession;
        how he sacrificed his wife and children
    how the world, so invasive, disappears
        when he leans over
           to line up a shot.

Nickel-and-Diming

In the winter of 1973,
Wally The Whale woke up in Maine,
playing 6-ball against
the owner of some
hole-in-the-wall pool room
for fifteen cents a rack.

Even though Wally kept winning,
the guy wouldn't up the ante or quit.
"Ain't got no wheres to be,"
the owner said as he chalked up.

Marvin Gaye's "Let's Get It On"
played at least five times an hour,
taunting the lonely men
who shuffled in and out.

Since according to house rules
winner couldn't walk, Wally stayed.
Even after 99 racks, when the locals
gathered around the table
like a lifetime of regrets
and the numbers on the balls
all became somehow symbolic
to Wally's life:

> 6 children
> 2 lost to death
> 4 lost respect for him
> 1 addict
> 5 times his wife took him back
> 3 flings during this road trip

Eventually, one by one, the men left,
like the balls rubbing their sleepy eyes
across the felt before being pocketed.
Finally, the owner broke down his stick.

"Guess it's bout quitting time," he said,
making his way to a bottle of whiskey
hidden beneath the register.

He poured two shots before
dumping nineteen dollars
and thirty-five cents in nickels and dimes
into Wally's sagging hands.

Fathers and Sons

"At the gambling table, there are no fathers and sons."
—*Chinese Proverb*

While other fathers rolled up their sleeves
to push papers, products, or politics,
Wally put a day's work in at the local pool hall,
breaking for a quick snack or a liquid lunch.

Because these days his reputation precedes him
and the game's not what it once was,
he subsidizes: dry walls, paints,
fences and runs books in between practices.

Every night, he used to moonlight:
throwing dice or cards in the musty basement
of some seedy establishment after close,
or sometimes in bed with a broad or two;
but now he's home on time for dinner
and for his wife, who waited out the years.

Back when he only came home for breakfast,
reeking of indecency, Wally put on kitchen mitts
and let his children box into them while his wife
fried eggs uneasily in haunting silence.

That's when Tommy and Danny fell in love
with taking swings at their father. Later, both boys
got caught up in their own diamonds as baseball players,
following Wally's applicable pool advice:
Look at the ball, but don't take your eyes off the players.

At first, Wally put money on Tommy's raw talent,
but when Tommy threw down his bat
for the needle, he became as invisible
to Wally as all of Wally's own mistakes.
Against the odds, Danny went pro.
Nowadays, he's the one ducking Wally
because he can't help but picture
his mother's tears falling softly onto runny yolks
and because his adversary has always been
-the man wearing those greasy kitchen mitts.

89

Fallen Cold and Dead

With Respect to Walt Whitman

Three bullets extracted from her body
were placed in a plastic bag, in a box, on a shelf
locked in a room and labeled 35 mm.

Wally shoots the six in the side,
triggers back the cue ball precisely
for the seven in the corner, half past

the eight, uneasy like there are waves
beneath the felt and the second hand,
he chokes, "Muthah fucking table's not level."

Has the ship "weather'd every rack"?

I heard, after his youngest daughter's murder,
Wally gave up the game for months;
steadfast, like Lincoln's stovepipe hat,
he rested on a bar stool until last call.

Chicken Chow Mein

I.

Wally The Whale paces outside the pool hall.
It's three minutes past noon
and he's pissed because he's old school:
"If you say you're open at noon
then you open at noon";
but he won't say that to me,
he'll just mumble inaudibly
until he gets over it.
I'll turn up the heat and the jazz
then wait on the coffee and Wally.

II.

Wally holds grudges the way my father did,
silently. Sometimes I convince myself
that's what stopped my father's heart,
but that's not altogether true.
When I got kicked out of high school,
my father punched a door,
broke his wrist, then fell silent.
It took him years to come around,
so I'm accustomed to waiting.

III.

I like Wally because he thinks
before he speaks and lives by his word.
Sometimes I run down the block
to get Chinese takeout,
leaving him, a known thief,
without suspicion to tend the register.
I trust him more, in that way,
than I trust some relatives.

And I like Wally because
he tells me stories about his son,
a famous baseball player,
and his oldest daughter,
a Hollywood lawyer.

IV.

Most of all, I like Wally
because it's Wednesday afternoon
and even though he's still pissy
at me for opening late
and annoyed that his table is slanted funny,
we're eating lukewarm chicken chow mein
that tastes like shit
with sloppy conversation and chopsticks
and he is the closest
I've been to my father
since he passed away
three long, quiet years ago.

The Shadow Cast By His Cue

My father taught me how to play pool
in the back room of some smoky dive
on a Sunday afternoon when I was a teenager.

In between lessons and anecdotes,
he let me take sips from his beer.

Even though, my father's only hustle
was a hard day's work, I can't help but see
his spirit in Wally The Whale—

something about the eyes, deeper than
cartilage and bone, more complex than language.

So when Wally shows me how
to steady my bridge, use the diamonds like maps,
and listen to the table, I hear my father—

something like a whisper, a shadow cast
by his cue, deafening like the memory
of a loved one buried below the surface.

Stretching Felt Over the Edges

for Mark

For decades, Wally caromed
from one one-night stand to the next
while his wife waited out the years,
faithful like a porch light,
fifty-five years and counting
burnt-out bulbs. Their love
pulled tight like felt
stretched over a billiard table.

Lately our conversations are
punctuated with doubt and suspicion.
Over 9-ball, we discuss divorce,
how three couples we know
are separating. Our failures, illness,
and miscues are disruptions,
slight wrinkles in the felt
altering the course balls travel.

Ten, twenty, thirty, forty, fifty,
years from now, will I wake up
beside you, the faint smell
of gamble lingering on your
pillowcase? Or will each crease
be a disappointment, changing the way
we travel toward one another?

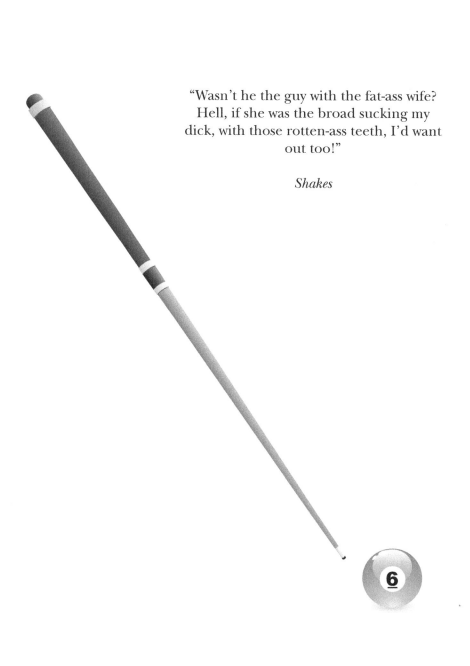

"Wasn't he the guy with the fat-ass wife?
Hell, if she was the broad sucking my
dick, with those rotten-ass teeth, I'd want
out too!"

Shakes

A Recession of the Heart

for Terry

Rain and the Dow Jones fell
relentlessly for three consecutive days.
No one at the pool hall
realized you were missing;
if they did, they didn't say so.
Mostly people complained
about the cost of living, the weather,
the way the balls rolled for them.
People take shelter in the chambers
of their own receding hearts.

On Monday, someone stole
the hand soap from the bathroom.
On Tuesday, Bernacke shook
his rain-stick tongue announcing
federal cuts for short-term lending.
On Wednesday, a wolf in a wool sweater
came in itching for a money game;
Mikey convinced him he was a little pig
then made some brick off of him.

Earlier today, Old Two-Shoes,
the crazy woman
who wears mismatched flats,
stood outside the pool hall
on the yellow dividing line,
waving her umbrella at oncoming traffic,
screaming: "Evacuate, evacuate,
this world is drowning in injustice."
The cops that took her away
chuckled as they locked her in.

Today, I overhear two people
arguing over whether your death
was a suicide, heart attack or overdose.

When they come up to pay,
they're three dollars short,
but promise they'll come right back.
After they leave, I fish through
a pile of old newspapers,
in search of answers, only to find out
who you really were from your obituary.

God Wind

for Terry

At the bar,
eleven days
before your suicide,
your wife drank
two pitchers
of kamikazes
as if fueling up.

Over the collision
of pool balls,
I heard her warn you:
"Terry, I can't go on
dying here with you."

Later she ran the table,
winning three games
in a row.
You watched,
slumped over
your woes, clumsily
bouncing up and down
as if caught
in turbulence.

When she ordered
another pitcher,
she sat across from me
to confess
she was moving
home to Louisiana.
You didn't know.

Two hours before her flight,
she told you
she was leaving

for good,
but you could sell
her belongings
to the pay bills.

The last time
I saw you,
you handed me
a gold name-plate necklace
that says Rachel.
I let you shoot pool
for free, watched you
stumble in and out
of the bathroom
and around the tables
shivering like a leaf
divorced from a tree.

Closed Casket & One Pocket

for Terry

I.

Since a plane ticket cost too much,
        your ex-wife stayed in Louisiana;
                with her new life
                        already underway,
                                on the day of your funeral,
                        she interviewed
                for a cashier position
        at the local mini-mart
then drank twelve beers.

With nothing left
        to drink,
                she stumbled back
                        to the mini-mart
        for a second interview
                that didn't go as well.

II.

Since no one sent flowers,
                the owner of the funeral parlor
        placed dusty, plastic arrangements
                around your closed casket.

The next morning, the manager phoned your ex-wife
        to tell her that she didn't get the job
                and that she owes the store
                        for the beef jerky sticks
        the surveillance camera caught her slipping into her pocket.

We didn't even know
        you died,
                so we played one pocket
                        until night closed the lid on day.

Pocket Full of Sadness

for Terry

For weeks,
while you made up
your mind,
you carried a loaded gun
in your winter coat.

Unknowingly,
I let you hold
my infant daughter,
run your fingers
through her fine hair,
whisper into her ear.

"As soon as those hairy-legged dykes got the right to vote, it was all over."

Mikey Meatballs

Cadillac Women

Fold time in half, midnight: laundry,
dusting, crocheting. Cold pot roast, carrots,
and potatoes asleep under plastic wrap.
Blue, volume-less, cob-webbed vows,
television glowing, crickets. Waiting.

Once, before "I do's," they believed
that union, routine, children, and church
would replace less attractive rituals.
How can six pockets and fifteen balls
steal decades from a man's life?

The ones who stayed, without expectations,
iron the wind's collared shirts, scrub the
crevices of longing with retired toothbrushes,
sweep truth underneath rent-to-own furniture
and shake out muddy rugs with frustrations.

Others, equally as insane as their men,
let their husbands parade around in dirty clothes,
let dust collect like unpaid bills, shun
domestic drudgery and practice a policy of:
microwave your own goddamn food.

The ones who escape wince
and hold their breath every time
they pass a pool hall as if it were a graveyard;
each table a burial plot, waiting to be filled, and
Cadillacs, reminders of what they couldn't change.

Tombstones, shovels, cue sticks. Nine balls racked:
the only diamond their husbands couldn't pawn.
Years of wanting and waiting have worn
creases into their felt faces. Their fears chipped
out their husband's epitaphs into the slate underneath.

What We Pray For

For over a decade,
all Wally's wife wanted
was a new vacuum cleaner
that would pick up crumbs
the first time around.

Finally on the morning
of their thirtieth anniversary,
Wally staggered in
pushing a fenced vacuum
with a red ribbon tied,
crookedly, to the handle.

By the end of the week,
the new vacuum,
in the back of the closet,
was an unanswered prayer.

The return of stubborn crumbs,
more faithful than her husband,
were welcomed back
without question.

Windows

It's been months,
but Old Two-Shoes resurfaces,
wearing the same outfit
she was taken away in,
down to the umbrella.

She looks into the pool hall window
as if she's staring down
a complex equation.
With her free hand,
on the glass,
she traces a figure.
She talks to this person,
rubs its hair
then kisses its forehead.

I wonder who the mystery person is:
a lover, a parent, a child?

The men inside don't look up
from their tables.
They draw balls back into pockets;
they kiss rails;
they bank on winning this one.

It's not raining;
it's not even cloudy out,
but her umbrella is open.

Just like with Terry,
no one missed her when she was gone.
The market did what the market does.
Gas rose and people complained.
Food costs rose and people complained.
The balls on the table rolled
where the balls will roll.

When I go outside to sneak a smoke,
she is still there,
looking through her imaginary friend,
whispering and smiling.

Abruptly, she backs away,
waves and points her umbrella
at the pool hall window:
"You can't eat my heart with chopsticks," she screams.
Then she moves to the next storefront
and places her greasy finger on the window.

Abstract of Woman with Pool Cue

The regulars on the front table
reminisce about all the pool halls
they've played in over the years
as if they were women
they've made love to.

"Damn," Shakes shouts,
"more pool halls have closed
their legs on me than women."

Later, I overhear
Mikey Meatballs's commentary
on women who chalk up:
"Next thing you know,
they'll want to use our urinals too!"

A few hours later, I hear Mikey ask:
"How many women does it take
to hold a pool cue?"
Unfortunately, the punch line's
muffled by the Cadillac Men's
premature laughter.

Old School Chat Rooms

Like their counterparts,
Cadillac Women have their
own language that
hasn't evolved too much
over the years.

Proof of this can be found
most often under paint
or wallpaper, but sometimes
in plain sight in the dingiest
of dives where women
feel the need to share
their most intimate sins.

In one such place, etched into
a bathroom stall I discovered
the "not so secret" secret:
*I speared Wally The Whale
on 7/11/88.* It was signed
with the moniker, *Moby Cunt.*

Playing the Table

"Before you can conquer the three rebellious ivory balls and make them do your bidding, you must first conquer yourself. I have found billiards to be more than a game; I have found it to be a philosophy of self-control."

                                        —*Willie Hoppe*

You tell me to play the table,
not my opponent,
but I can't help thinking
about the shot I just missed,
how my jeans, too tight,
rub my surgical scar raw,
about essays I have to grade
when I get home tonight,
and how the only time
you talk to me lately
is to, in great detail,
explain what I could do better.

I'm not good at being
in the here and now;
what was and what will be
hang over the table
like a swaying brass light
casting shadows
over my shots.
The felt turns into a mirror—
and I can't help
looking up at myself
as I lean into the table.
I consider how
I am not the woman
you or I want me to be.

I miss the bank,
usually an effortless make,

the woman we want me to be
wouldn't have missed.
She would have led the cue back
to center table as if it were
a leashed white poodle.
Then she would have made
the seven in the side
and the four
in the corner
with enough follow
to set up perfectly
for the eight, but I am not
that woman.

Instead I second-guess shots,
leave myself nothing
then get frustrated
when you repeat yourself,
"Play the table, not your opponent."
Because futile thoughts
skip like scratched records,
I doubt the philosophy
of self-control,
know that my only solace
will forever be buried
deep within the silent pauses
of poems and understand
men that choose the stick
over the constraints of convention.

Eight Legs in 8-Ball

The fly, a drunken old man,
staggers through the air,
trips over stubborn wings,
bumps into this and that
before becoming tangled
in a web stretched between
two dusty copper lampshades
that hang above a pool table.

Below, Patty, Mikey Meatballs's,
latest ex-wife, breaks
then runs four low balls.
As each nears a pocket,
she wiggles her sixty-year-old ass
and shouts "Get legs, get legs!"
She's been around a lot lately
since the loneliness of routine
bullied her into taking Mikey back.

Outside, three teenagers
push a stalled car
to the side of the street.
One of them lifts the hood,
then looks inside.
Behind them, Old Two-Shoes
rocks back and forth
on tippy-toes, trying to get
a glimpse of their secret.
When they turn around,
she disappears.

I wonder if Patty
told her girlfriends
about how she lets the man
who held a gun to her head
and clocked her in the face
with a pool ball,

sleep on her pull-out sofa
after he's done fucking her.
If she did, she probably
prefaced the news with:
But he's different.

The next time I look out the window,
the boys and their car are gone,
but Old Two-Shoes is back
standing where they once stood,
hunched over and looking into
the hood of her imagination.
She fiddles with invisible wires,
trying to figure out what's gone wrong.

The fly stops struggling
and waits for death's eight legs
to wrap around him.
Mikey lets Patty win,
he slaps her ass and says:
"That's my patty-cake."
She smiles and shakes her ass.

Because a spider's web is translucent,
Patty is tangled up in the moment.

Marked

The last time I saw Rita,
she was standing outside
the beauty parlor talking
to Mikey Meatballs.

The word is Wheels
never did buy that ring;
he got mugged
that same night when
Rita climbed up
onto his handle bars.

The word is
after he dropped Rita off,
two guys pushed him
off his bike,
beat him senseless,
took his money,
and stomped his
bicycle wheels.

After that Wally The Whale
refused to play Mikey,
never said why, never had to,
he was still cordial,
the way an old school hustler
is known to be
even after a fellow
crosses the line.

Too Late in the Game

for Mark

On our third "date," at our favorite dive,
you played eight-ball with the bartender
for ten dollars a rack.

That night after the bar,
we stopped at the gas station
and I suggested you buy some lotto tickets
since you were so lucky on the table.

You laughed and said,
"I only take calculated risks."

We went back to your place,
had sex, ate hot dogs on paper plates
and watched the sun come up.

You told me you thought you could love me
and I said I know what you mean.
I was too drunk and tired
to ask about the calculated risks.

"Man, I don't want life to hustle me out of what is mine like it did to Bobby Balls-In-Hand. I am going to get the money for that ring again, no matter what it takes. Then I am going to get Rita back."

Wheels aka Spanish Fly

When Almost All of the Balloons Are Popped

After spending two hours
in the emergency room
waiting for our daughter's diagnosis—
allergic reaction to amoxicillin—
I ice fifteen birthday cupcakes
to look like a rack of pool balls
for her first birthday party.

After most of the balloons pop,
the presents are opened,
the flame stolen from the wick
of a single pink candle,
and all the guests are back
to their own lives;
Mark tells me that Bobby Balls-In-Hand
was given three weeks to live.

Since there isn't much
worth discussing,
Mark racks and I break.
When the door opens,
the few remaining balloons sway
like the unsettled feeling in my stomach.

Foreign Languages

Pool halls were once meeting places
where men went to escape their wives,
children and to-do lists.

"Remember when men were men?"
Mikey asks the other Cadillac Men
after a thin goth boy wearing black lipstick
walks out of the pool hall
with a laptop under his arm.

The goth boy doesn't come for pool;
he uses our wireless Internet connection,
and sips herbal tea by the front window.
He doesn't look up from his screen,
but smiles every now and then
interacting with his computer
like the Cadillac Men socialize with one another.

"These kids today don't even talk no more,"
Shakes says after a ten-ball run,
"they just play on those stupid machines."

"The only thing computers are good for is porn,"
Mikey says.

"But the best part of porn's feeling the pages
between your fingers,"
Bobby Balls-In-Hand sets himself up,
but the men let it go
because prostate cancer's punishment enough.

None of the Cadillac Men own computers.
Their keyboard's a Brunswick
and their mouse a Balabushka.
Their language may be misunderstood,
but it is their language,
and besides their lavish pool sticks,
it is the only thing they own outright.

Expiration Date

You place an egg in a glass of water;
since it doesn't float, you fetch a frying pan.

Like the egg, Bobby Balls-In-Hand is two weeks
and three days past his given expiration date,
but unlike the egg, he floats above his days.

Now that conversation and money
are useless currencies, he has more of both.

Ambivalently, he told you he's spent more time
battling cancer than cradling his daughter;
now he's too estranged for apologies.

From the Inside Out

A shovel turns over dirt
like men turn over decisions.

Without apologies traded
between old friends,
Bobby Balls-In-Hand was buried
on a Wednesday afternoon.

No one will ever know
how Shakes mourned
thirty-five years of friendship
lost
on an icy afternoon
over a ball
frozen against a rail.

From the Outside In

Bobby's daughter stood
beside his casket
to see him for the first time.

Rumor is he left her everything:
a hand-carved pool stick,
a wallet full of stake money,
his '73 Cadillac
with a glove box full
of unpaid parking tickets.

We Inherited a Sense of Loss

What we want to say is tangled around
our tongues like Bobby's red scarf
wrapped around the leg of the front table.

Winter and Bobby have passed;
so has hope of profit
and our faith in one another.

We have inherited his red scarf,
a pool hall full of mourners;
a huge debt and a sense of loss
that we can't talk about yet.

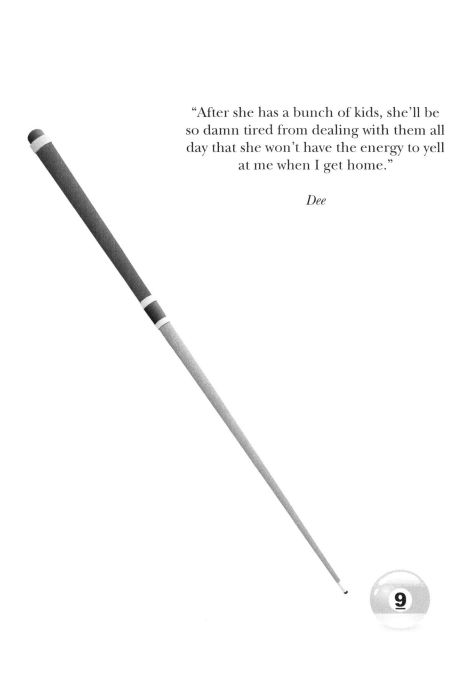

"After she has a bunch of kids, she'll be so damn tired from dealing with them all day that she won't have the energy to yell at me when I get home."

Dee

Pool Time

There are no seasons
                inside this cave,
no ornate snowflakes,
        no crocuses,
                no summer squash blossoms,
                        no rusty autumn leaves,
just hustlers,
            thieves,
                junkies,
                    and ball-bangers
etching their tales
        into the dusty air
like instruments
        fighting
                the gravity
                    of impermanence
because like jazz musicians
        pool junkies move
                at their own speed;
                    they keep playing
until the muse
        breaks
                and runs
                    them out.

The Equestrian in the Can

The smell of fish walks in ten minutes before Aristotle.

After he says hello, he turns around Miles Davis–style,
with his back to me. He runs his long slender fingers
across the table's felt as if it were a parallel universe,
a rabbit hole, a trap door that he could escape through.

He wears his shame on his dirty white T-shirt, ripped
and speckled with shiny silver fish scales.

He won't tell me that he's been back on the horse
for months now, instead he loses his balance,
catches himself on the rail with one hand,
leaves it there like his actions were intentional.

Then after a few seconds, he makes the other hand
a fist that he presses against his lips;
he blows his words through it as if it were a trumpet:
"The transmission dropped out of my heart;
someone stole the kickstand from my fishing pole,
so I'm wearing out the tires they took from me, spiritually.
I just can't look into the tables; they're crystal balls."

After a few seconds of silence, he disappears
into the bathroom. A new group of men come in,
they play six racks of eight-ball before one of them tries
the bathroom door again. He stands there knocking,
then asks: "Is someone dead in there?"

For a minute or two, I think about the possibility.

But then Aristotle emerges, zig-zags around the tables,
past the men who cringe as he swims past them.
Slowly Aristotle moves toward the front doors,
heavy at the hooves, yet light at the mane,
and pushes out into the streets without a goodbye.

Going Out for Ice Cream

Dee has eighty-nine dollars
until next Friday
and is playing Mikey Meatballs for a hundred.
Dee's wife's been calling him all night;
she's waiting for the ice cream
she sent him out for.
She's eight-and-a-half months pregnant
and bursting with expectations.

But tonight, Dee's happy
because he's schooling
one of the Cadillac Men
and he's cocky, really cocky,
telling Mikey he's washed up.

What Dee doesn't know
is that Mikey's just reeling him in;
that the night his wife's water breaks,
he'll be down three hundred more
than he has in his wallet;
that in twenty years
he'll be a Cadillac Man too,
with his own moniker:
Dee-vorced
because his wife will have long since
melted out of his life
like the mint chocolate chip ice cream
that never found its way home.

Nice Touch

"Fear can make a sucker do some of the most drastic
things you ever imagined…like taking a job."
                              —*Minnesota Fats, 1966*

Dee stomps into the pool hall
wearing a work-shirt,
his name embroidered in blue
above his left breast pocket.

Mikey snickers, "So is it the wife
or fear that got to ya?"

Without answering, Dee walks
into the bathroom and comes out
with his shirt turned inside out.

"Dee, you should've left it.
It really adds a nice touch.
If I were a few pounds lighter,
I'd borrow it for my trip
down to Tampa this weekend."

Mister Ding-a-ling-a-ling

Nostalgia's a rocket pop:
red, white and blue,
summer nights, loose change
in sweaty pockets.

Nostalgia will be different
for the teens, who invent
new rules while they play
eight-ball on the back table

and brazenly discuss how,
last night, they smoked
Mister Ding-a-ling-a-ling up
for a ride down Broadway.

While music blared in unison
with children's pleas for:
Ice cream! Ice cream!
I-c-e c-r-e-a-mmmm!

Popsicles, the high, and their
youth all melted in their mouths
as the truck zig-zagged sloppily
over the yellow dividing lines.

Swimming Lessons

It's so hot, people stop in, buy a cold soda
and sit at the front tables. No one plays pool
but Wheels, who has a sweat-soaked red bandana
wrapped around his forehead.
I suck on ice cubes
while Mark fiddles with the temperamental AC.
He still hasn't stopped believing everything is fixable.

Outside Old Two-Shoes is in the middle of the road,
teetering on the yellow line.
She's wearing a blue bathing suit,
which is decorated with colorful tropical fish
and her usual mismatched flats.
She is doing the breast stroke as passing cars honk.

The people at the front table are unfazed,
this is Kingston and we all know it,
so we go about our business
and every once in a while we all look out
to see if Old Two-Shoes is still giving swimming lessons.

The Storm Turns

The storm turns, the way a man does
when his wife loses faith in him.

The Butcher and Dee play one pocket
on a table with felt that is as worn out
as their hearts. The slate, and their mistakes
peek out, redirecting balls traveling through.

Lately my fears solidify, a hailstorm
of insults that shift to a warmth of regret.

The Butcher's up forty points
and three decades of disappointments,
but Dee gambles in his shadow,
walks his walk, talks his talk.

By default Dee's married to the rain,
a furious wife, beating down
on her husband's concrete shoulders.

Real Estate

When the day doesn't work out
the way it should,
I think of the Cadillac Men
and where they were
twenty, thirty, forty, fifty years ago.

I picture a dark, musty pool room
with concrete floors and curtained windows
where smoke and trash talk billow
from mouths and twist in the air
above the next shot, waiting.

That smoke and trash talk
still linger between the same
four yellow-stained walls,
even though the pool tables
have been replaced by office desks
and men who work on commissions.

How effortlessly 9-5ers replace
Cadillac Men without remorse
in the same vein
Pilgrims did Indians.
Pool cues turn into ballpoint pens,
bows and arrows into muskets.

How quickly men sell
each square foot of their souls
for the right price,
even if it means subdividing.
The Cadillac Men
battle with cue and stick
against the times.
They will never admit the land
will always belong to the men
with the bloodiest hands.

Playing Down for Shakes

Shakes used to run fifty balls
without blinking
before the wear and tear
of the years caught up with him.

Word around Crazy Eights is his moniker
was The Surgeon, decades ago,
due to his precision on the table.
Now his fingers fumble
when putting lids on coffee cups.

Most guys will only play Shakes
for old time's sake, table time,
coffee, a good story or a few bucks.

That's what some Cadillac Men
do for one another,
it's an amendment
to their unwritten constitution,
a break away from hustling.

They know Shakes will bet
all he's got bar his vintage Caddy,
even though he can barely
run a rack on a good day.
They know he will leave sulking
after an inevitable loss.

They know Wally The Whale's eyesight
is his most daunting opponent,
that sometimes he whispers
to his ghost daughter
who he believes watches him play.

When Bobby Balls-In-Hand's days
were numbered they reminisced
about the good ole days,

and fell silent when he asked
if he should call his daughter.

They've witnessed Aristotle get on
and off the horse a hundred times
and Mikey Meatballs's mental breaks,
divorces and countless schemes.
They know who to go to
for what and when.

They know Shakes
will play Mikey Meatballs
no matter how many times
they warn him not to.
They knew The Butcher
when he was the man to know.

Some of them placed bets
on how much Dee would weigh
when he was born.
Wally The Whale and The Butcher
were the last to see Dee's father
the night his car collided
with a bread delivery truck.

They were all there the night
someone poured sugar
into Mikey Meatballs's gas tank
and he came in yelling
about how he was gonna slit
the fucker's throat.
Suspiciously, they all
eyeballed one another.
That was before
The Butcher's divorce,
Wally's first heart attack,
and even before
Dee was allowed to drink legally.

136

Now they all know Mark's hustle,
how he plays down for all the men,
how he lets them win
so they feel better about themselves
and stick around longer.
They all know that's not enough
to keep a pool hall going in this town.

All of them, except Wheels, know
what Rita did for Mikey Meatballs.
They know why Patty wore sunglasses
for a few weeks and they all predicted
that she would come back anyway.
They have all come to accept
Old Two-Shoes as part of the landscape.
Knowing that I play pool like shit,
they all play down for me too;
because to some of them,
I am the daughter that they lost or abandoned.
To the others, I am a woman
who will sacrifice everything for my man.

"Worrying about the future won't change it; all you'll do is waste energy."

Mark

First Steps

Our daughter
        takes her first steps
                between us
                        on a Sunday morning
                                at the pool hall
        as the Cadillac Men
                shuffle in
                        like a royal flush.

We clap
        she claps
                and the Cadillac Men clap.

For the first time
        in weeks,
                it doesn't matter
        that we know we have to close the pool hall,
        that we are living on credit cards,
        or that the only words
                we exchange lately
                        are insults;

because right now
        we're all smiling
                as our daughter
                steadies herself on the pool table,
                        turns around
                                and takes a few more steps.

Whisper

"Whisper," you say,
        "no one needs to know
                about our shortcomings,"
especially
No That Pocket George
            who plays straight pool
                against a bottle,
                    sheltered in a wrinkled
                brown paper bag
or our daughter
        who sleeps in her stroller
            below the empty register.

You haven't slept in 47 hours
or eaten in 18,
so you're dizzy, tired,
and nervous that I'll ask you what we're going to do now.

Another Casualty

Wally The Whale's favorite watering hall closed down two weeks ago,
but if you don't look closely as you pass, you won't notice;
the sign, still there, says open; the same old men lean against the brick building
smoking cigarettes and bullshitting; the traffic still stops at the light
when it's red and still moves on when it's green.
The only thing missing is Wally's white Cadillac sitting faithfully at the curb.

Growing Up

Not long after we closed the pool hall,
I stand behind Aristotle at the gas station.
He leans into the counter
with his right hand bridged
as if his fingers are molded for a cue stick.
Out loud, he debates whether to buy a cherry Phillies blunt
or try the tequila flavored.

"Go with what you can depend on," I say.
Without turning around, I hear his lips crack into a smile,
"Eh, Beck, yup, I'll go cherry."
Without looking at me, he turns
and says, "Bet the lil' one's all grown up by now."

I consider how two months can seem like decades;
how our daughter is beginning to string words together logically;
how Mark's hair has become more gray than brown;
and how his laugh lines have atrophied along with my expectations.

"Yes, I have," I slip as he navigates around me:
like time, he rushes out the door without looking back.

Dee-cisions

Dee waved to me the other day
as I drove by the women's clinic;
he was standing beside his car
holding hands with some chick.
She was facing the dedicated man,
holding a sign that displayed
a mangled fetus
and a caption that read:
7th Week Aborted.

I wonder if he promised
to bring her out for ice cream after.

Going Back

Mark goes back to the pool hall
for the mail,
everything else is in storage,
except the lone beverage machine
that the company never came back for,
glowing in the darkness
of our abandoned dream.

Besides bills and a letter from the IRS,
he finds a note written on a napkin
from Mikey Meatballs that reads:
Mark, give me a call
337-2389 Mikey Meatballs.

Mark told me he tossed the note,
but I find it
in the back pocket of his jeans
on laundry day.

After his jeans are washed
and dried, I fold the napkin
and place it back
where I found it.

Brake Lights

Some small businesses weather the recession black market style
others just disappear, abandoning their fancy signs and dreams.
Today the rain turned to snow then back again. Tomorrow, you will

scramble eggs, look for a job, winterize the house. Yesterday
you put the pool tables into storage, lifted twenty-four
three hundred pound slates onto dollies then pushed them across

slippery sidewalks into a moving truck. Since there's no time to
mourn our losses, I fix dinner, bathe our daughter, put her to bed
before taking three times the recommended dosage of sleeping pills.

I walk a dog that we don't own around a neighborhood that we don't live in.
I sit across the street from the building where our pool hall was,
but don't look directly into it. So much is in need of repair: our water heater,

the brakes on both of our cars, our credit card debt, and the not-so-subtle way
we blame one another. One Cadillac passes by slowly, then another and
another. A white Cadillac circles back around the block and parks.

Wally The Whale gets out and puts his face to the windows; he doesn't notice me.
When he gets back into his car and pulls away, I wonder where he's going;
where he will end up; if we will find our way back to one another?

My eyelids are heavy like Wally's foot on the brake as he drifts down Broadway.
I guess we're both trying to figure out what to do next. I am afraid this is the last
I will see of Wally The Whale, his Cadillac's red eyes blinking as he drives away.

"Someone asked me why women don't gamble as much as men do, and I gave the commonsensical reply that we don't have as much money. That was a true and incomplete answer. In fact, women's total instinct for gambling is satisfied by marriage."

Gloria Steinem

Next Time

for Mark

Eight months after closing the pool hall, the first night in two years
we are without our daughter, we celebrate our fifth wedding anniversary.

You suggest we walk down to the Esopus Creek, even though it's raining.
We share one umbrella and when I slip on wet pavement you catch me.

At a restaurant we can only afford because of a gift certificate, I order
lobster and you order prime rib; we substitute dessert for another round of

draft beers. We watch raindrops merge with the creek water and debate
whether the fifth-year anniversary gift should be wood or silverware.

You laugh when I slip the rest of the dinner bread in my bag for
the ducks; we are trying to collect what we can from what we lost.

After dinner, we find a dive with a pool table. It's been months since
I've agreed to play. You rack, I break, and before the eight drops

I am in love with the game again. Later as we stumble alongside the creek,
I pull out a gold name-plate necklace that says Rachel and the bread

from my purse to toss into the Esopus. We are holding hands again and
talking, really talking since we left the bar. As we watch the necklace sink,

you say you saw a building in another town, perfect for a pool hall,
and we start to discuss how we'll do it differently next time.

Photo by Karen Calabria

Rebecca Schumejda is the author of *Falling Forward*, (sunnyoutside, 2009); *From Seed to Sin* (Bottle of Smoke Press, 2011), *The Map of Our Garden* (verve bath, 2009); *Dream Big, Work Harder* (sunnyoutside, 2006); and *The Tear Duct of the Storm* (Green Bean Press, 2001).

She received her MA in Poetics and Creative Writing from San Francisco State University and her BA in English and Creative Writing from SUNY New Paltz. She lives in New York's Hudson Valley with her husband and daughter.

The New York Quarterly Foundation, Inc.

New York, New York

Poetry
Magazine

Since 1969

Edgy, fresh, groundbreaking, eclectic—voices from all walks of life.

Definitely NOT your mama's poetry magazine!

The *New York Quarterly* has been defining the term contemporary American poetry since its first craft interview with W. H. Auden.

Interviews • Essays • and of course, lots of poems.

www.nyquarterly.org

No contest! That's correct, NYQ Books are NO CONTEST to other small presses because we do not support ourselves through contests. Our books are carefully selected by invitation only, so you know that NYQ Books are produced with the same editorial integrity as the magazine that has brought you the most eclectic contemporary American poetry since 1969.

Books

nyqbooks.org

poetry at the edge™

CPSIA information can be obtained at www.ICGtesting.com
Printed in the USA
LVOW011105171012

303204LV00007B/1/P